NUWAVE

Air Fryer Cookbook for Beginners

Foolproof, Quick and Easy Recipes to Master Your Nuwave Air Fryer Like a Pro

Air Fryer Lab

Table of Content

BREAKFAST 7

   1.   CHOCOLATE PEANUT BUTTER BREAD..8
   2.   HEARTY BLUEBERRY OATMEAL 10
   3.   PROTEIN EGG CUPS 12
   4.   PUMPKIN PANCAKES 14
   5.   SHRIMP FRITTATA 16
   6.   TUNA SANDWICHES 18
   7.   SHRIMP SANDWICHES..20
   8.   CHICKEN & ZUCCHINI OMELET 21

MAIN DISHES 23

   9.   SLOPPY JOES...24
  10. BROCCOLI BEEF...26
  11. KOREAN BEEF BOWL 28
  12. MONGOLIAN BEEF AND BROCCOLI..30
  13. ALL-IN-ONE MEATLOAF WITH MASHED POTATOES.........................32
  14. HAWAIIAN PINEAPPLE PORK 34
  15. CLASSIC MEDITERRANEAN QUICHE..36
  16. GOLDEN SPRING ROLLS..38

MEAT & POULTRY 41

  17. TURKEY AND PEPPER SANDWICH 42
  18. SPICY TURKEY BREAST 44
  19. CHICKEN, MUSHROOM, AND PEPPER KABOBS 46
  20. CHICKEN & ZUCCHINI 48
  21. CHICKEN QUESADILLA...50
  22. BUFFALO CHICKEN WINGS 52
  23. SEASONED PORK TENDERLOIN..54
  24. GARLICKY PORK TENDERLOIN 56
  25. GLAZED PORK TENDERLOIN 57
  26. COUNTRY STYLE PORK TENDERLOIN 59

FISH & SEAFOOD 61

  27. PARMESAN AND PAPRIKA BAKED TILAPIA 62
  28. TANGY COD FILLETS 64
  29. FISH AND CAULIFLOWER CAKES 65
  30. MARINATED SCALLOPS WITH BUTTER AND BEER 67
  31. CHEESY FISH GRATIN..68
  32. FIJIAN COCONUT FISH 70
  33. SOLE FISH AND CAULIFLOWER FRITTERS 72

VEGETABLE, SOUP & STEW 75

34. RUSSET POTATOES WITH YOGURT AND CHIVES 76
35. GOLDEN SQUASH CROQUETTES 77
36. GOLDEN CHEESY CORN CASSEROLE 79
37. BREADED CHEESY BROCCOLI GRATIN 81
38. BROCCOLI WITH HOT SAUCE 83
39. CRISPY BRUSSELS SPROUTS WITH SAGE 85
40. AIR FRYER MINESTRONE SOUP 87
41. AIR FRYER GREEK BEEF STEW 89
42. AIR FRYER BEAN SOUP 91

SNACK & DESSERT 93

43. CHEESY GARLIC SWEET POTATOES 94
44. CRISPY GARLIC BAKED POTATO WEDGES 95
45. STICKY CHICKEN THAI WINGS 97
46. COCONUT SHRIMP 99
47. SPICY KOREAN CAULIFLOWER BITES 101
48. MINI POPOVERS 103
49. LEMON PEAR COMPOTE 104
50. STRAWBERRY STEW 106

MEASUREMENT CONVERSION CHART 109

Breakfast

1. Chocolate Peanut Butter Bread

Preparation Time: 15 minutes

Cooking Time: 30 minutes

Servings: 8

Ingredients:

- ¾ cup all-purpose flour

- ¼ cup cocoa powder

- ¼ cup sugar

- ½ teaspoon baking soda

- ½ teaspoon baking powder

- 1/8 teaspoon salt

- 1 egg

- 1/3 cup unsweetened applesauce

- ¼ cup plain Greek yogurt

- ½ teaspoon vanilla extract

- 1/3 cup creamy peanut butter

- 1/3 cup mini chocolate chips

Directions:

1. In a bowl, mix together the flour, cocoa powder, sugar, baking soda, baking powder, and salt.

2. In another bowl, add the egg, applesauce, yogurt, and vanilla extract. Beat until well combined.

3. Then, add in the flour mixture and mix until just combined.

4. Add the peanut butter and mix until smooth.

5. Gently, fold in the chocolate chips.

6. Set the temperature of Air Fryer to 350 degrees F. Grease a loaf pan.

7. Place the mixture evenly into the prepared pan.

8. Arrange the loaf pan into an Air Fryer basket.

9. Air Fry for about 30 minutes or until a toothpick inserted in the center comes out clean.

10. Remove from Air Fryer and place the pan onto a wire rack for about 10-15 minutes.

11. Carefully, take out the bread from pan and put onto a wire rack until it is completely cool before slicing.

12. Cut the bread into desired size slices and serve.

Nutrition: Calories: 191 Carbohydrate: 24.9g Protein: 6.1g Fat: 8.6g Sugar: 12.6g Sodium: 183mg

2. Hearty Blueberry Oatmeal

Preparation Time: 10 minutes

Cooking Time: 25 minutes

Servings: 6

Ingredients:

- 1½ cups quick oats
- 1¼ teaspoons ground cinnamon, divided
- ½ teaspoon baking powder
- Pinch salt
- 1 cup unsweetened vanilla almond milk
- ¼ cup honey
- 1 teaspoon vanilla extract
- 1 egg, beaten
- 2 cups blueberries
- Olive oil
- 1½ teaspoons sugar, divided
- 6 tablespoons low-fat whipped topping (optional)

Directions:

1. In a large bowl, mix together the oats, 1 teaspoon of cinnamon, baking powder, and salt.

2. In a medium bowl, whisk together the almond milk, honey, vanilla and egg.

3. Pour the liquid ingredients into the oats mixture and stir to combine. Fold in the blueberries.

4. Lightly spray a round air fryer–friendly pan with oil.

5. Add half the blueberry mixture to the pan.

6. Sprinkle ⅛ teaspoon of cinnamon and ½ teaspoon sugar over the top.

7. Cover the pan with aluminum foil and place gently in the fryer basket. Air fry for 20 minutes remove the foil and air fry for an additional 5 minutes Transfer the mixture to a shallow bowl.

8. Repeat with the remaining blueberry mixture, ½ teaspoon of sugar, and ⅛ teaspoon of cinnamon.

9. To serve, spoon into bowls and top with whipped topping.

Nutrition: Calories 170 Fat 3g Saturated Fat 1g Cholesterol 97mg Carbs 34g Protein 4g Fiber 4g Sodium: 97mg

3. Protein Egg Cups

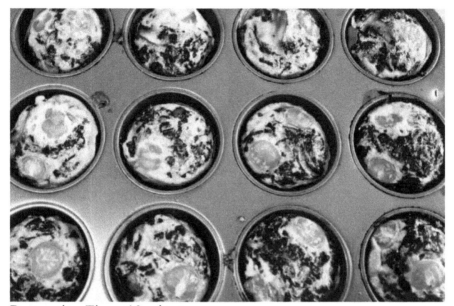

Preparation Time: 10 minutes

Cooking Time: 9 minutes

Servings: 2

Ingredients:

- 3 eggs, lightly beaten
- 4 tomato slices
- 4 tsp cheddar cheese, shredded
- 2 bacon slices, cooked and crumbled
- Pepper
- Salt

Directions:

1. Spray silicone muffin molds with cooking spray.

2. In a small bowl, whisk the egg with pepper and salt.

3. Preheat the air fryer to 350 F. Pour eggs into the silicone muffin molds.

4. Divide cheese and bacon into molds.

5. Top each with tomato slice and place in the air fryer basket. Cook for 9 minutes.

6. Serve and enjoy.

Nutrition: Calories 67 Fat 4 g Carbohydrates 1 g Sugar 0.7 g Protein 5.1 g Cholesterol 125 mg

4. Pumpkin Pancakes

Preparation Time: 15 minutes

Cooking Time: 12 minutes

Servings: 2

Ingredients:

- 1 square puff pastry
- 3 tablespoons pumpkin filling
- 1 small egg, beaten

Directions:

7. Roll out a square of puff pastry and layer it with pumpkin pie filling, leaving about ¼-inch space around the edges. Cut it up into 8 equal sized square pieces and coat the edges with beaten egg.

8. Press "Power Button" of Air Fry Oven and turn the dial to select the "Air Fry" mode.

9. Press the Time button and again turn the dial to set the cooking time to 12 minutes.

10. Now push the Temp button and rotate the dial to set the temperature at 355 degrees F. Press "Start/Pause" button to start.

11. When the unit beeps to show that it is preheated, open the lid.

12. Arrange the squares into a greased "Sheet Pan" and insert in the oven.

13. Serve warm.

Nutrition: Calories 109 Total Fat 6.7 g Saturated Fat 1.8 g Cholesterol 34 mg Sodium 87 mg Total Carbs 9.8 g Fiber 0.5 g Sugar 2.6 g Protein 2.4 g

5. Shrimp Frittata

Preparation time: 10 minutes

Cooking time: 15 minutes

Servings: 2

Ingredients:

- 4 eggs
- ½ teaspoon basil, dried
- Cooking spray
- Salt and black pepper to the taste
- ½ cup rice, cooked
- ½ cup shrimp, cooked, peeled, deveined and chopped
- ½ cup baby spinach, chopped

- ½ cup Monterey jack cheese, grated

Directions:

1. In a bowl, mix eggs with salt, pepper and basil and whisk.

2. Grease your air fryer's pan with cooking spray and add rice, shrimp and spinach.

3. Add eggs mix, sprinkle cheese all over and cook in your air fryer at 350 degrees F for 10 minutes.

4. Divide among plates and serve for breakfast.

5. Enjoy!

Nutrition: Calories 162 Fat 6 Fiber 5 Carbs 8 Protein 4

6. Tuna Sandwiches

Preparation time: 10 minutes

Cooking time: 5 minutes

Servings: 2

Ingredients:

- 16 ounces canned tuna, drained
- ¼ cup mayonnaise
- 2 tablespoons mustard
- 1 tablespoons lemon juice
- 2 green onions, chopped
- 3 English muffins, halved
- 3 tablespoons butter
- 6 provolone cheese

Directions:

6. In a bowl, mix tuna with mayo, lemon juice, mustard and green onions and stir.

7. Grease muffin halves with the butter, place them in preheated air fryer and bake them at 350 degrees F for 4 minutes.

8. Spread tuna mix on muffin halves, top each with provolone cheese, return sandwiches to air fryer and cook them for 4 minutes, divide among plates and serve for breakfast right away.

9. Enjoy!

Nutrition: Calories: 182 Fat: 4 Fiber: 7 Carbs: 8 Protein: 6

7. Shrimp Sandwiches

Preparation time: 10 minutes

Cooking time: 5 minutes

Servings: 2

Ingredients:

- 1 and ¼ cups cheddar, shredded
- 6 ounces canned tiny shrimp, drained
- 3 tablespoons mayonnaise
- 2 tablespoons green onions, chopped
- 4 whole wheat bread slices
- 2 tablespoons butter, soft

Directions:

1. In a bowl, mix shrimp with cheese, green onion and mayo and stir well.
2. Spread this on half of the bread slices, top with the other bread slices, cut into halves diagonally and spread butter on top.
3. Place sandwiches in your air fryer and cook at 350 degrees F for 5 minutes.
4. Divide shrimp sandwiches on plates and serve them for breakfast.
5. Enjoy!

Nutrition: Calories: 16 Fat: 3 Fiber: 7 Carbs: 12 Protein: 4

8. Chicken & Zucchini Omelet

Preparation Time: 15 minutes

Cooking Time: 35 minutes

Servings: 2

Ingredients:

- 8 eggs
- ½ cup milk
- Salt and ground black pepper, as required
- 1 cup cooked chicken, chopped
- 1 cup Cheddar cheese, shredded
- ½ cup fresh chives, chopped
- ¾ cup zucchini, chopped

Directions:

1. In a bowl, add the eggs, milk, salt and black pepper and beat well. Add the remaining ingredients and stir to combine.

2. Place the mixture into a greased baking pan. Press "Power Button" of Air Fry Oven and turn the dial to select the "Air Bake" mode. Press the Time button and again turn the dial to set the cooking time to 35 minutes.

3. Now push the Temp button and rotate the dial to set the temperature at 315 degrees F. Press "Start/Pause" button to start.

4. When the unit beeps to show that it is preheated, open the lid. Arrange pan over the "Wire Rack" and insert in the oven.

5. Cut into equal-sized wedges and serve hot.

Nutrition: Calories: 209 Total Fat: 13.3 g Saturated Fat: 6.3 g Cholesterol: 258 mg Sodium: 252 mg Total Carbs: 2.3 g Fiber: 0.3 g Sugar: 1.8 g Protein: 9.8 g

Main Dishes

9. Sloppy Joes

Preparation Time: 5 minutes

Cooking Time: 15 minutes

Servings: 8

Ingredients:

- 1 tablespoon extra-virgin olive oil

- 2 pounds 90% lean ground beef

- 1 teaspoon onion powder

- ½ teaspoon garlic powder

- 1 teaspoon chili powder

- 1 (16-ounce) can tomato purée

- ½ cup ketchup

- 2 tablespoons reduced-sodium soy sauce

- 1 tablespoon brown sugar

- Purple slaw, for garnish (optional)

- Fresh chopped parsley, for garnish (optional)

Directions:

1. Choose Sauté and add the olive oil to the inner pot. Once the oil is warm enough, addthe ground beef and cook for 3 minutes, using a spatula for crumbling the meat.

2. Press Cancel and add the onion powder, garlic powder, chili powder, tomato purée, ketchup, soy sauce, and brown sugar. Stir to combine.

3. Secure the lid into place. Choose Pressure Cook or Manual; fix the pressure toHigh and the time to 10 minutes. Ensure the steam release knob is in the sealed position. Once done cooking, release the pressure naturally for 10 minutes, then quick release the remaining pressure.

4. Open the lid. Stir the Sloppy Joe mixture to make sure it's well mixed.

5. Serve immediately garnished with purple slaw and parsley, if desired, or place the Sloppy Joes in an airtight container and refrigerate for up to 4 days or freeze for up to 2 months.

Nutrition: Calories 246 Protein 24 g. Fat 12 g. Carbs 7 g.

10.   Broccoli Beef

Preparation Time: 20 minutes

Cooking Time: 19 minutes

Servings: 6

Ingredients:

- 2 tablespoons cornstarch

- ½ cup water

- 1 tablespoon extra-virgin olive oil

- 2 pounds flank steak, cut into ½-inch-thick slices

- 3 garlic cloves, minced

- ½ cup low-sodium beef broth

- ⅓ cup reduced-sodium soy sauce

- ¼ cup white wine vinegar

- 1 tablespoon brown sugar

- 2 teaspoons Sriracha sauce

- ¼ teaspoon ground ginger

- 1 pound broccoli florets, fresh or frozen (about 3½ cups)

- 4 scallions, sliced, for garnish

Directions:

1. In a bowl, create a slurry by mixing the water and cornstarch together. Set aside.

2. Choose Sauté and add the olive oil to the inner pot. Once the oil is warm enough, addthe steak and garlic and sauté for 3 minutes, stirring once in a while so the beef starts to brown on both sides.

3. Press Cancel and add the broth. Using a wooden spoon, remove any browned bits stuck to the bottom of the pot. Add the soy sauce, vinegar, brown sugar, Sriracha, and ginger; stir to combine.

4. Secure the lid into place. Choose Pressure Cook or Manual; fix the pressure toHigh and the time to 8 minutes. Ensure the steam release knob is in the sealed position. Once done cooking, naturally release the pressure for 5 minutes, then quick release any remaining pressure.

5. Unlock and remove the lid. Add the broccoli florets.

6. Lock the lid into place again. Choose Pressure Cook or Manual; fix the pressure to High and the time to 1 minute. Ensure the steam release knob is in the sealed position. Once done cooking, quick release the pressure.

7. Open the lid. Choose Sauté. Use a slotted spoon to transfer the beef and broccoli to a serving plate.

8. Once the liquid is bubbling in the inner pot, whisk in the cornstarch slurry and let the sauce cook, uncovered, for 2 minutes or until it starts to thicken.

9. Return the beef and broccoli to the pot and stir to combine.

10. Serve the dish garnished with the scallions

Nutrition: Calories 330 Protein 35 g. Fat 16 g. Carbs 10 g.

11. Korean Beef Bowl

Preparation Time: 15 minutes

Cooking Time: 20 minutes

Servings: 6

Ingredients:

- 2 tablespoons cornstarch
- ½ cup water
- 1 tablespoon extra-virgin olive oil
- 2 pounds flank steak, sliced into ½-inch-thick strips
- 3 garlic cloves, minced
- ½ cup low-sodium beef broth
- ⅓ cup reduced-sodium soy sauce
- ¼ cup white wine vinegar
- 2 tablespoons honey
- 2 teaspoons Sriracha sauce
- ¼ teaspoon ground ginger
- 1 medium cucumber, sliced
- 2 red bell peppers, seeded and sliced
- 4 scallions, sliced

Directions:

1. In a bowl create a slurry by whisking the water and cornstarchtogether. Reserve.

2. Choose Sauté and add the olive oil to the inner pot. Once the oil is warm enough, addthe steak and garlic and sauté for 3 minutes, stirring occasionally so the beef starts to brown on all sides.

3. Choose Cancel then add the broth. Using a wooden spoon, remove any browned bits stuck to the bottom of the pot. Add the vinegar, soy sauce, Sriracha,honey, and ginger; stir to combine.

4. Secure the lid into place. Choose Pressure Cook or Manual; fix the pressure toHigh and the time to 10 minutes. Ensure the steam release knob is in the sealed position. Once done cooking, release the pressure naturally for 5 minutes, then quick release any remaining pressure.

5. Unlock and remove the lid. Select Sauté. Use a slotted spoon to transfer the beef to a serving plate.

6. Once the liquid begins to bubble, whisk in the cornstarch slurry and let the sauce cook, uncovered, for 2 minutes or until it starts to thicken. Place the beef back to the pot and stir to combine.

7. Serve every bowl with a few slices of cucumber and red bell pepper and some sliced scallions on top.

Nutrition: Calories 355 Protein 36 g. Fat 16 g. Carbs 16 g.

12. Mongolian Beef And Broccoli

Preparation Time: 10 minutes

Cooking Time: 16 minutes

Servings: 6

Ingredients:

- 2 tablespoons cornstarch

- ½ cup water

- 2 tablespoons extra-virgin olive oil

- 1 medium yellow onion, chopped

- 2 pounds skirt steak, cut into strips

- 2 garlic cloves, minced

- 1 cup low-sodium beef broth

- ¼ cup reduced-sodium soy sauce

- 2 tablespoons balsamic vinegar

- 2 tablespoons brown sugar

- 15 ounces broccoli florets, fresh or frozen

Directions:

1. In a bowl, create a slurry by whisking together the cornstarch and water. Set aside.

2. Choose Sauté and add the olive oil. Once the oil is hot enough, add the steak, onion, and garlic; cook for about 3 minutes, stirring occasionally.

3. Press Cancel and add the broth, soy sauce, vinegar, and brown sugar; stir to combine. Using a wooden spoon, remove any browned bits stuck to the bottom of the pot.

4. Secure the lid into place. Choose Pressure Cook or Manual; fix the pressure toHigh and the time to 10 minutes. Ensure the steam release knob is in the sealed position. Once done cooking, naturally release the pressure for 5 minutes, then quick release any remaining pressure.

5. Unlock and remove the lid. Add the broccoli florets.

6. Lock the lid into place again. Choose Pressure Cook or Manual; set the pressure to High and the time to 1 minute (3 minutes if using frozen florets). Ensure the steam release knob is in the sealed position. Once done cooking, quick release the pressure.

7. Open the lid. Choose Sauté. Use a slotted spoon to transfer the beef and vegetables to a serving bowl.

8. Whisk the cornstarch slurry into the liquid. Let it cook, uncovered, for 2 minutes or until the sauce starts to thicken. Press Cancel. Add the beef and vegetables into the pot and stir to combine.

9. Serve immediately, or place the beef and vegetables in a sealed container and refrigerate for up to 4 days or freeze for up to 2 months.

Nutrition: Calories 321 Protein 37 g. Fat 14 g. Carbs 10 g.

13.　All-In-One Meatloaf with Mashed Potatoes

Preparation Time: 10 minutes

Cooking Time: 30 minutes

Servings: 8

Ingredients:

- 1 pound medium russet or Yukon Gold potatoes
- 1 cup low-sodium chicken broth
- 2 pounds 90% lean ground beef
- ½ medium yellow onion, chopped
- 2 garlic cloves, minced
- 1 egg
- 2 teaspoons Worcestershire sauce

- 1 teaspoon Dijon mustard

- 2 tablespoons unsalted butter

- 1 teaspoon fine sea salt

- ½ teaspoon freshly ground black pepper

Directions:

1. Place the potatoes and broth in the inner pot.

2. In a bowl, mix the ground beef, onion, garlic, egg, Worcestershire sauce, and mustard. Using your hands, combine the ingredients together thoroughly.

3. Form the meatloaf mixture into a loaf that will fit inside the inner pot.

4. Tear off a 2-foot piece of aluminum foil and fold it in half. Turn up the edges so it makes the shape of a square basket that will fit inside the inner pot. Place the meatloaf in the foil basket and place it on top of the potatoes.

5. Secure the lid into place. Choose Pressure Cook or Manual; fix the pressure toHigh and set to 30 minutes. Ensure the steam release knob is in the sealed position. Once done cooking, naturally release the pressure for 10 minutes, then quick release the remaining pressure.

6. Unlock and remove the lid. Carefully remove the meatloaf and the foil from the pot. Add the butter, salt, and pepper to the potatoes, then mash them to your liking with a potato masher or immersion blender.

7. Serve immediately, or place the meatloaf and mashed potatoes in separate airtight containers and refrigerate for up to 4 days or freeze for up to 2 months.

Nutrition: Calories 286 Protein 25 g. Fat 14 g. Carbs 12 g.

14.   Hawaiian Pineapple Pork

Preparation Time: 10 minutes

Cooking Time: 15 minutes

Servings: 6

Ingredients:

- 2 tablespoons extra-virgin olive oil

- 2 lbs. pork loin, cut into 1-inch cubes

- 1 medium yellow onion, chopped

- 3 garlic cloves, minced

- 1 (20-ounce) can pineapple chunks in juice

- 2 red bell peppers, seeded and chopped

- ¼ cup reduced-sodium soy sauce

- 2 tablespoons brown sugar

- ¼ teaspoon chili powder

Directions:

1. Choose Sauté and add the olive oil to the inner container. Once the oil is hot enough, add the pork, onion, and garlic; sauté for 4 minutes, stirring occasionally to brown the pork on all sides.

2. Press Cancel and add the pineapple and its juice. Using a wooden spoon, remove any browned bits stuck to the bottom of the pot. Add the bell peppers, soy sauce, brown sugar, and chili powder. Stir to combine.

3. Secure the lid into place. Choose Pressure Cook or Manual; fix the pressure to High and the time to 10 minutes. Ensure the steam release knob is in the sealed position. Once done cooking, naturally release the pressure for 10 minutes, then quick release any remaining pressure.

4. Open the lid. Serve immediately, or place the pork and vegetables in an airtight container and refrigerate for up to 4 days.

Nutrition: Calories 343 Protein 30 g. Fat 16 g. Carbs 23 g.

15. Classic Mediterranean Quiche

Preparation Time: 10 minutes

Cooking Time: 30 minutes

Servings: 4

Ingredients:

- 4 eggs

- ¼ cup chopped Kalamata olives

- 1/2 cup chopped tomatoes

- ¼ cup chopped onion

- 1/2 cup milk

- 1 cup crumbled feta cheese

- 1/2 tablespoon chopped oregano

- 1/2 tablespoon chopped basil

- Salt and ground black pepper, to taste

- Cooking spray

Directions:

1. Spritz a baking pan with cooking spray.

2. Whisk the eggs with remaining ingredients in a large bowl. Stir to mix well.

3. Pour the mixture into the prepared baking pan.

4. Place the pan on the bake position.

5. Select Bake, set temperature to 340°F (171°C) and set time to 30 minutes.

6. When cooking is complete, the eggs should be set and a toothpick inserted in the center should come out clean.

7. Serve immediately.

Nutrition: Calories 246 Carbs 0.1g Fat 2.8g Protein 10.8g

16. Golden Spring Rolls

Preparation Time: 10 minutes

Cooking Time: 18 minutes

Servings: 4

Ingredients:

- 4 spring roll wrappers

- 1/2 cup cooked vermicelli noodles

- 1 teaspoon sesame oil

- 1 tablespoon freshly minced ginger

- 1 tablespoon soy sauce

- 1 clove garlic, minced

- 1/2 red bell pepper, deseeded and chopped

- 1/2 cup chopped carrot

- 1/2 cup chopped mushrooms

- ¼ cup chopped scallions

- Cooking spray

Directions:

1. Spritz the air fry basket with cooking spray and set aside.

2. Heat the sesame oil in a saucepan on medium heat. Sauté the garlic and ginger in the sesame oil for 1 minute, or until fragrant. Add soy sauce, carrot, red bell pepper, mushrooms and scallions. Sauté for 5 minutes or until the vegetables become tender. Mix in vermicelli noodles. Turn off the heat and remove them from the saucepan. Allow to cool for 10 minutes.

3. Lay out one spring roll wrapper with a corner pointed toward you. Scoop the noodle mixture on spring roll wrapper and fold corner up over the mixture. Fold left and right corners toward the center and continue to roll to make firmly sealed rolls.

4. Arrange the spring rolls in the basket and spritz with cooking spray.

5. Place the basket on the air fry position.

6. Select Air Fry, set temperature to 340°F (171°C) and set time to 12 minutes. Flip the spring rolls halfway through the cooking time.

7. When done, the spring rolls will be golden brown and crispy.

8. Serve warm.

Nutrition: Calories 242 Carbs 0.1g Fat 2.8g Protein 6.8g

Meat & Poultry

17.   Turkey And Pepper Sandwich

Preparation Time: 5 minutes

Cooking Time: 5 minutes

Servings: 1

Ingredients:

- 2 slices whole grain bread

- 2 teaspoons Dijon mustard

- 2 ounces (57 g) cooked turkey breast, thinly sliced

- 2 slices low-fat Swiss cheese

- 3 strips roasted red bell pepper

- From the Cupboard:

- Salt and ground black pepper, to taste

Directions:

1. Preheat the air fryer to 330°F (166°C). Spritz the air fryer basket with cooking spray.

2. Assemble the sandwich: On a dish, place a slice of bread, then top the bread with 1 teaspoon of Dijon mustard, use a knife to smear the mustard evenly.

3. Layer the turkey slices, Swiss cheese slices, and red pepper strips on the bread according to your favorite order. Top them with remaining teaspoon of Dijon mustard and remaining bread slice.

4. Place the sandwich in the preheated air fryer and spritz with cooking spray. Sprinkle with salt and black pepper.

5. Cook for 5 minutes until the cheese melts and the bread is lightly browned. Flip the sandwich halfway through the cooking time.

6. Serve the sandwich immediately.

Nutrition: Calories: 328 Fat: 5.0g Carbs: 38.0g Protein: 29.0g

18. Spicy Turkey Breast

Preparation Time: 5 minutes

Cooking Time: 40 minutes

Servings: 4

Ingredients:

- 2-pound (907 g) turkey breast

- 2 teaspoons taco seasonings

- 1 teaspoon ground cumin

- 1 teaspoon red pepper flakes

- From the Cupboard:

- Salt and ground black pepper, to taste

Directions:

- Preheat the air fryer to 350°F (180°C). Spritz the air fryer basket with cooking spray.

- On a clean work surface, rub the turkey breast with taco seasoning, ground cumin, red pepper flakes, salt, and black pepper.

- Arrange the turkey in the preheated air fryer and cook for 40 minutes or until the internal temperature of the turkey reads at least 165°F (74°C). Flip the turkey breast halfway through the cooking time.

- Remove the turkey from the basket. Allow to cool for 15 minutes before slicing to serve.

Nutrition: Calories: 235 Fat: 5.6g Carbs: 6.6g Protein: 37.3g

19.   Chicken, Mushroom, And Pepper Kabobs

Preparation Time: 1 hour 5 minutes

Cooking Time: 15-20 minutes

Servings: 4

Ingredients:

- ⅓ cup raw honey

- 2 tablespoons sesame seeds

- 2 boneless chicken breasts, cut into cubes

- 6 white mushrooms, cut in halves

- 3 green or red bell peppers, diced

From the Cupboard:

- ⅓ cup soy sauce

- Salt and ground black pepper, to taste

- Special Equipment:

- 4 wooden skewers, soaked for at least 30 minutes

Directions:

1. Combine the honey, soy sauce, sesame seeds, salt, and black pepper in a large bowl. Stir to mix well.

2. Dunk the chicken cubes in this bowl, then wrap the bowl in plastic and refrigerate to marinate for at least an hour.

3. Preheat the air fryer to 390°F (199°C). Spritz the air fryer basket with cooking spray.

4. Remove the chicken cubes from the marinade, then run the skewers through the chicken cubes, mushrooms, and bell peppers alternatively.

5. Baste the chicken, mushrooms, and bell peppers with the marinade, then arrange them in the preheated air fryer.

6. Spritz them with cooking spray and cook for 15 to 20 minutes or until the mushrooms and bell peppers are tender and the chicken cubes are well browned. Flip them halfway through the cooking time.

7. Transfer the skewers to a large plate and serve hot.

Nutrition: Calories: 380 Fat: 16.0g Carbs: 26.1g Protein: 34.0g

20. Chicken & Zucchini

Preparation Time: 30 minutes

Cooking Time: 20 minutes

Servings: 6

Ingredients:

- 1/4 cup olive oil
- 1 tablespoon lemon juice
- 2 tablespoons red wine vinegar
- 1 teaspoon oregano
- 1 tablespoon garlic, chopped
- 2 chicken breast fillet, sliced into cubes
- 1 zucchini, sliced
- 1 red onion, sliced
- 1 cup cherry tomatoes, sliced
- Salt and pepper to taste

Directions:

1. In a bowl, mix the olive oil, lemon juice, vinegar, oregano and garlic.
2. Pour half of mixture into another bowl.
3. Toss chicken in half of the mixture.
4. Cover and marinate for 15 minutes.
5. Toss the veggies in the remaining mixture.
6. Season both chicken and veggies with salt and pepper.

7. Add chicken to the air fryer basket.

8. Spread veggies on top.

9. Select air fry function. Seal and cook at 380 degrees f for 15 to 20 minutes.

Nutrition: Calories: 282 kcal Protein: 21.87 g Fat: 19.04 g Carbohydrates: 5.31 g

21. Chicken Quesadilla

Preparation Time: 20 minutes

Cooking Time: 30 minutes

Servings: 8

Ingredients:

- 4 tortillas

- Cooking spray

- 1/2 cup sour cream

- 1/2 cup salsa

- Hot sauce

- 12 oz. chicken breast fillet, chopped and grilled

- 3 jalapeño peppers, diced

- 2 cups cheddar cheese, shredded

- Chopped scallions

Directions:

1. Add grill grate to the Air Fryer Oven. Close the hood. Choose grill setting and preheat for 5 minutes.

2. While waiting, spray tortillas with oil.

3. In a bowl, mix sour cream, salsa and hot sauce. Set aside.

4. Add tortilla to the grate. Grill for 1 minute.

5. Repeat with the other tortillas.

6. Spread the toasted tortilla with the salsa mixture, chicken, jalapeño peppers, cheese and scallions.

7. Place a tortilla on top. Press.

8. Repeat these steps with the remaining 2 tortillas.

9. Take the grill out of the pot. Choose roast setting.

10. Cook the Quesadillas at 350F for 25 minutes.

Nutrition: Calories:184 kcal Protein: 12.66 g Fat: 7.66 g Carbohydrates: 15.87 g

22. Buffalo Chicken Wings

Preparation Time: 15 minutes

Cooking Time: 30 minutes

Servings: 4

Ingredients:

- 2 lb. chicken wings
- 2 tablespoons oil
- 1/2 cup Buffalo sauce

Directions:

1. Coat the chicken wings with oil.
2. Add these to an air fryer basket.
3. Choose air fry function.
4. Cook at 390 degrees F for 15 minutes.

5. Shake and then cook for another 15 minutes.

6. Dip in Buffalo sauce before serving.

Nutrition: Calories: 376 kcal Protein: 51.93 g Fat: 16.4 g Carbohydrates: 2.18 g

23. Seasoned Pork Tenderloin

Preparation Time: 10 minutes

Cooking Time: 45 minutes

Servings: 5

Ingredients:

- 1½ pounds pork tenderloin

- 2-3 tablespoons BBQ pork seasoning

Directions:

1. Rub the pork with seasoning generously. Insert the rotisserie rod through the pork tenderloin.

2. Insert the rotisserie forks, one on each side of the rod to secure the pork tenderloin.

3. Arrange the drip pan in the bottom of Air Fryer Oven cooking chamber.

4. Select "Roast" and then adjust the temperature to 360 degrees F.

5. Set the timer for 45 minutes and press the "Start".

6. When the display shows "Add Food" press the red lever down and load the left side of the rod into the Air Fryer Oven.

7. Now, slide the rod's left side into the groove along the metal bar so it doesn't move.

8. Then, close the door and touch "Rotate".

9. Press the red lever to release the rod when cooking time is complete.

10. Remove the pork and place onto a platter for about 10 minutes before slicing.

11. With a sharp knife, cut the roast into desired sized slices and serve.

Nutrition: Calories 195 Fat 4.8 g Carbs 0 g Protein 35.6 g

24. Garlicky Pork Tenderloin

Preparation Time: 15 minutes

Cooking Time: 20 minutes

Servings: 5

Ingredients:

- 1½ pounds pork tenderloin
- Nonstick cooking spray
- 2 small heads roasted garlic
- Salt and ground black pepper, as required

Directions:

1. Lightly, spray all the sides of pork with cooking spray and then, season with salt and black pepper.

2. Now, rub the pork with roasted garlic. Arrange the roast onto the lightly greased cooking tray.

3. Arrange the drip pan in the bottom of Air Fryer Oven cooking chamber.

4. Select "Air Fry" and then adjust the temperature to 400 degrees F. Set the timer for 20 minutes and press the "Start".

5. When the display shows "Add Food" insert the cooking tray in the center position.

6. When the display shows "Turn Food" turn the pork.

7. When cooking time is complete, remove the tray and place the roast onto a platter for about 10 minutes before slicing. With a sharp knife, cut the roast into desired sized slices and serve.

Nutrition: Calories 202 Fat 4.8 g Carbs 1.7 g Protein 35.9 g

25. Glazed Pork Tenderloin

Preparation Time: 15 minutes

Cooking Time: 20 minutes

Servings: 3

Ingredients:

- 1-pound pork tenderloin
- 2 tablespoons Sriracha
- 2 tablespoons honey
- Salt, as required

Directions:

1. Insert the rotisserie rod through the pork tenderloin.
2. Insert the rotisserie forks, one on each side of the rod to secure the pork tenderloin.
3. In a small bowl, add the Sriracha, honey and salt and mix well.

4. Brush the pork tenderloin with honey mixture evenly.

5. Arrange the drip pan in the bottom of Air Fryer Oven cooking chamber.

6. Select "Air Fry" and then adjust the temperature to 350 degrees F.

7. Set the timer for 20 minutes and press the "Start".

8. When the display shows "Add Food" press the red lever down and load the left side of the rod into the Oven.

9. Now, slide the rod's left side into the groove along the metal bar so it doesn't move.

10. Then, close the door and touch "Rotate".

11. Press the red lever to release the rod when cooking time is complete.

12. Remove the pork and place onto a platter for about 10 minutes before slicing.

13. With a sharp knife, cut the roast into desired sized slices and serve.

Nutrition: Calories 269 Fat 5.3 g Carbs 13.5 g Protein 39.7 g

26. Country Style Pork Tenderloin

Preparation Time: 15 minutes

Cooking Time: 25 minutes

Servings: 3

Ingredients:

- 1-pound pork tenderloin
- 1 tablespoon garlic, minced
- 2 tablespoons soy sauce
- 2 tablespoons honey
- 1 tablespoon Dijon mustard
- 1 tablespoon grain mustard
- 1 teaspoon Sriracha sauce

Directions:

1. In a large bowl, add all the ingredients except pork and mix well.

2. Add the pork tenderloin and coat with the mixture generously.

3. Refrigerate to marinate for 2-3 hours.

4. Remove the pork tenderloin from bowl, reserving the marinade.

5. Place the pork tenderloin onto the lightly greased cooking tray.

6. Arrange the drip pan in the bottom of Air Fryer Oven cooking chamber.

7. Select "Air Fry" and then adjust the temperature to 380 degrees F.

8. Set the timer for 25 minutes and press the "Start".

9. When the display shows "Add Food" insert the cooking tray in the center position.

10. When the display shows "Turn Food" turn the pork and oat with the reserved marinade.

11. When cooking time is complete, remove the tray and place the pork tenderloin onto a platter for about 10 minutes before slicing.

12. With a sharp knife, cut the pork tenderloin into desired sized slices and serve.

Nutrition: Calories 277 Fat 5.7 g Carbs 14.2 g Protein 40.7 g

Fish & Seafood

27. Parmesan and Paprika Baked Tilapia

Preparation time: 20 minutes

Cooking time: 15 minutes

Servings: 6

Ingredients:

- cup parmesan cheese, grated

- 1 teaspoon paprika

- 1 teaspoon dried dill weed

- pounds tilapia fillets

- 1/3 cup mayonnaise

- 1/2 tablespoon lime juice

- Salt and ground black pepper, to taste

Directions

1. Mix the mayonnaise, parmesan, paprika, salt, black pepper, and dill weed until everything is thoroughly combined.

2. Then, drizzle tilapia fillets with the lime juice.

3. Cover each fish fillet with parmesan/mayo mixture; roll them in parmesan/paprika mixture. Bake at 335 for about 10 minutes. Serve and eat warm.

Nutrition: 294 calories 16.1g fat 2.7g carbs 35.9g protein 0.1g sugars 0.2g fiber

28.   Tangy Cod Fillets

Preparation time: 20 minutes

Cooking time: 15 minutes

Servings: 2

Ingredients:

- ½ tablespoons sesame oil

- 1/2 heaping teaspoon dried parsley flakes

- 1/3 teaspoon fresh lemon zest, finely grated

- medium-sized cod fillets

- 1 teaspoon sea salt flakes

- A pinch of salt and pepper

- 1/3 teaspoon ground black pepper, or more to savor

- 1/2 tablespoon fresh lemon juice

Directions

1. Set the air fryer to cook at 375 degrees f. Season each cod fillet with sea salt flakes, black pepper, and dried parsley flakes. Now, drizzle them with sesame oil.

2. Place the seasoned cod fillets in a single layer at the bottom of the cooking basket; air-fry approximately 10 minutes.

3. While the fillets are cooking, prepare the sauce by mixing the other ingredients. Serve cod fillets on four individual plates garnished with the creamy citrus sauce.

Nutrition: 291 calories 11.1g fat 2.7g carbs 41.6g protein 1.2g sugars 0.5g fiber

29. Fish and Cauliflower Cakes

Preparation Time: 2 hours 20 minutes

Cooking Time: 13 minutes

Servings: 4

Ingredients:

- 1/2-pound cauliflower florets

- 1/2 teaspoon English mustard

- 2 tablespoons butter, room temperature

- 1/2 tablespoon cilantro, minced

- 2 tablespoons sour cream

- 2 ½ cups cooked white fish

- Salt and freshly cracked black pepper, to savor

Directions:

1. Boil the cauliflower until tender. Then, purée the cauliflower in your blender. Transfer to a mixing dish.

2. Now, stir in the fish, cilantro, salt, and black pepper.

3. Add the sour cream, English mustard, and butter; mix until everything's well incorporated. Using your hands, shape into patties.

4. Place in the refrigerator for about 2 hours. Cook for 13 minutes at 395 degrees f. Serve with some extra English mustard.

Nutrition: 285 calories 15.1g fat 4.3g carbs 31.1g protein 1.6g sugars 1.3g fiber

30. Marinated Scallops with Butter And Beer

Preparation Time: 1 hour 10 minutes

Cooking Time: 7 minutes

Servings: 4

Ingredients:

- 2 pounds sea scallops

- 1/2 cup beer

- 4 tablespoons butter

- 2 sprigs rosemary, only leaves

- Sea salt and freshly cracked black pepper, to taste

Directions

1. In a ceramic dish, mix the sea scallops with beer; let it marinate for 1 hour.

2. Meanwhile, preheat your air fryer to 400 degrees f. Melt the butter and add the rosemary leaves. Stir for a few minutes.

3. Discard the marinade and transfer the sea scallops to the air fryer basket. Season with salt and black pepper.

4. Cook the scallops in the preheated air fryer for 7 minutes, shaking the basket halfway through the cooking time. Work in batches.

Nutrition: 471 calories 27.3g fat 1.9g carbs 54g protein 0.2g sugars 0.1g fiber

31.   Cheesy Fish Gratin

Preparation Time: 30 minutes

Cooking Time: 20 minutes

Servings: 4

Ingredients:

1. tablespoon avocado oil

2. 1-pound hake fillets

3. 1 teaspoon garlic powder

4. Sea salt and ground white pepper, to taste

5. tablespoons shallots, chopped

6. 1 bell pepper, seeded and chopped

7. 1/2 cup cottage cheese

8. 1/2 cup sour cream

9. 1 egg, well whisked

10. 1 teaspoon yellow mustard

11. 1 tablespoon lime juice

12. 1/2 cup swiss cheese, shredded

Directions:

1. Brush the bottom and sides of a casserole dish with avocado oil. Add the hake fillets to the casserole dish and sprinkle with garlic powder, salt, and pepper.

2. Add the chopped shallots and bell peppers.

3. In a mixing bowl, thoroughly combine the cottage cheese, sour cream, egg, mustard, and lime juice. Pour the mixture over fish and spread evenly.

4. Cook in the preheated air fryer at 370 degrees f for 10 minutes.

5. Top with the Swiss cheese and cook an additional 7 minutes. Let it rest for 10 minutes before slicing and serving.

Nutrition: 335 calories 18.1g fats 7.8g carbs 33.7g protein 2.6g sugars 0.6g fiber

32. Fijian Coconut Fish

Preparation Time: 20 minutes + marinating time

Cooking Time: 15 minutes

Servings: 2

Ingredients:

- cup coconut milk
- tablespoons lime juice
- tablespoons shoyu sauce
- Salt and white pepper, to taste
- 1 teaspoon turmeric powder
- 1/2 teaspoon ginger powder
- 1/2 thai bird's eye chili, seeded and finely chopped
- 1-pound tilapia
- 2 tablespoons olive oil

Directions:

1. In a mixing bowl, thoroughly combine the coconut milk with the lime juice, shoyu sauce, salt, pepper, turmeric, ginger, and chili pepper. Add tilapia and let it marinate for 1 hour.

2. Brush the air fryer basket with olive oil. Discard the marinade and place the tilapia fillets in the air fryer basket.

3. Cook the tilapia in the preheated air fryer at 400 degrees f for 6 minutes; turn them over and cook for 6 minutes more. Work in batches.

4. Serve with some extra lime wedges if desired.

Nutrition: 426 calories 21.5g fat 9.4g carbs 50.2g protein 5g sugars 3.4g fiber

33. Sole Fish and Cauliflower Fritters

Preparation Time: 30 minutes

Cooking Time: 25 minutes

Servings: 2

Ingredients:

- 1/2 pound sole fillets
- 1/2 pound mashed cauliflower
- egg, well beaten
- 1/2 cup red onion, chopped
- garlic cloves, minced
- tablespoons fresh parsley, chopped
- 1 bell pepper, finely chopped
- 1/2 teaspoon scotch bonnet pepper, minced
- 1 tablespoon olive oil
- 1 tablespoon coconut aminos
- 1/2 teaspoon paprika
- Salt and white pepper, to taste

Directions:

1. Start by preheating your air fryer to 395 degrees f. Spritz the sides and bottom of the cooking basket with cooking spray.

2. Cook the sole fillets in the preheated air fryer for 10 minutes, flipping them halfway through the cooking time.

3. In a mixing bowl, mash the sole fillets into flakes. Stir in the remaining ingredients. Shape the fish mixture into patties.

4. Bake in the preheated air fryer at 390 degrees f for 14 minutes, flipping them halfway through the cooking time.

Nutrition: 322 calories 14g fat 27.4g carbs 22.1g protein 4.2g sugars 3.5g fiber

Vegetable, Soup & Stew

34. Russet Potatoes with Yogurt and Chives

Preparation Time: 5 minutes

Cooking Time: 35 minutes

Servings: 4

Ingredients:

- 4 (7-ounce / 198-g) russet potatoes, rinsed
- Olive oil spray
- 1/2 teaspoon kosher salt, divided
- 1/2 cup 2% plain Greek yogurt
- ¼ cup minced fresh chives
- Freshly ground black pepper, to taste

Directions:

1. Pat the potatoes dry and pierce them all over with a fork. Spritz the potatoes with olive oil spray. Sprinkle with ¼ teaspoon of the salt.

2. Transfer the potatoes to the air fry basket.

3. Place the basket on the bake position.

4. Select Bake, set temperature to 400°F (205°C), and set time to 35 minutes.

5. When cooking is complete, the potatoes should be fork-tender. Remove from the air fryer grill and split open the potatoes. Top with the chives, yogurt, the remaining ¼ teaspoon of salt, and finish with the black pepper. Serve immediately.

Nutrition: Calories 246 Carbs 0.1g Fat 2.8g Protein 10.8g

35. Golden Squash Croquettes

Preparation Time: 5 minutes

Cooking Time: 17 minutes

Servings: 4

Ingredients:

- 1/3 butternut squash, peeled and grated

- 1/3 cup all-purpose flour

- 2 eggs, whisked

- 4 cloves garlic, minced

- 1 1/2 tablespoons olive oil

- 1 teaspoon fine sea salt

- 1/3 teaspoon freshly ground black pepper, or more to taste

- 1/3 teaspoon dried sage

- A pinch of ground allspice

Directions:

1. Line the air fry basket with parchment paper. Set aside.

2. In a mixing bowl, stir together all the ingredients until well combined.

3. Make the squash croquettes: Use a small cookie scoop to drop tablespoonfuls of the squash mixture onto a lightly floured surface and shape into balls with your hands. Transfer them to the air fry basket.

4. Place the basket on the air fry position.

5. Select Air Fry, set temperature to 345°F (174°C), and set time to 17 minutes.

6. When cooking is complete, the squash croquettes should be golden brown. Remove from the air fryer grill to a plate and serve warm.

Nutrition: Calories 216 Carbs 0.1g Fat 3.8g Protein 10.8g

36.   Golden Cheesy Corn Casserole

Preparation Time: 5 minutes

Cooking Time: 15 minutes

Servings: 4

Ingredients:

- 2 cups frozen yellow corn
- 1 egg, beaten
- 3 tablespoons flour
- 1/2 cup grated Swiss or Havarti cheese
- 1/2 cup light cream
- ¼ cup milk
- Pinch salt
- Freshly ground black pepper, to taste
- 2 tablespoons butter, cut into cubes
- Nonstick cooking spray

Directions:

1.   Spritz a baking pan with nonstick cooking spray.

2.   Stir together the remaining ingredients except the butter in a medium bowl until well incorporated. Transfer the mixture to the prepared baking pan and scatter with the butter cubes.

3.   Place the pan on the bake position.

4.   Select Bake, set temperature to 320°F (160°C), and set time to 15 minutes.

5.   When cooking is complete, the top should be golden brown and a toothpick inserted in the center should come out clean. Remove the pan from the air fryer grill. Let the casserole cool for 5 minutes before slicing into wedges and serving.

Nutrition: Calories 257 Carbs 0.1g Fat 2.8g Protein 12.8g

37.   Breaded Cheesy Broccoli Gratin

Preparation Time: 5 minutes

Cooking Time: 14 minutes

Servings: 2

Ingredients

- 1/3 cup fat-free milk

- 1 tablespoon all-purpose or gluten-free flour

- 1/2 tablespoon olive oil

- 1/2 teaspoon ground sage

- ¼ teaspoon kosher salt

- 1/8 teaspoon freshly ground black pepper

- 2 cups roughly chopped broccoli florets

- 6 tablespoons shredded Cheddar cheese

- 2 tablespoons panko bread crumbs

- 1 tablespoon grated Parmesan cheese

- Olive oil spray

Directions:

1. Spritz a baking dish with olive oil spray.

2. Mix the milk, olive oil, flour, salt, sage, and pepper in a medium bowl and whisk to combine. Stir in the broccoli florets, bread crumbs, Parmesan cheese, and Cheddar cheese and toss to coat.

3. Pour the broccoli mixture into the prepared baking dish.

4. Place the baking dish on the bake position.

5.   Select Bake, set temperature to 330°F (166°C), and set time to 14 minutes.

6.   When cooking is complete, the top should be golden brown and the broccoli should be tender. Remove from the air fryer grill and serve immediately.

Nutrition: Calories 246 Carbs 0.1g Fat 2.8g Protein 10.8g

38. Broccoli with Hot Sauce

Preparation Time: 5 minutes

Cooking Time: 14 minutes

Servings: 6

Ingredients:

Broccoli:

- 1 medium-sized head broccoli, cut into florets
- 11/2 tablespoons olive oil
- 1 teaspoon shallot powder
- 1 teaspoon porcini powder
- 1/2 teaspoon freshly grated lemon zest

- 1/2 teaspoon hot paprika

- 1/2 teaspoon granulated garlic

- 1/3 teaspoon fine sea salt

- 1/3 teaspoon celery seeds

Hot Sauce:

- 1/2 cup tomato sauce

- 1 tablespoon balsamic vinegar

- 1/2 teaspoon ground allspice

Directions:

1. In a mixing bowl, combine all the ingredients for the broccoli and toss to coat. Transfer the broccoli to the air fry basket.

2. Place the basket on the air fry position.

3. Select Air Fry, set temperature to 360°F (182°C), and set time to 14 minutes.

4. Meanwhile, make the hot sauce by whisking together the balsamic vinegar, tomato sauce, and allspice in a small bowl.

5. When cooking is complete, remove the broccoli from the air fryer grill and serve with the hot sauce.

Nutrition: Calories 213 Carbs 0.1g Fat 2.8g Protein 8.3g

39. Crispy Brussels sprouts with Sage

Preparation Time: 5 minutes

Cooking Time: 15 minutes

Servings: 4

Ingredients:

- 1 pound (454 g) Brussels sprouts, halved
- 1 cup bread crumbs
- 2 tablespoons grated Grana Padano cheese
- 1 tablespoon paprika
- 2 tablespoons canola oil
- 1 tablespoon chopped sage

Directions:

1. Line the air fry basket with parchment paper. Set aside.

2. In a small bowl, thoroughly mix the cheese, bread crumbs, and paprika. In a large bowl, place the Brussels sprouts and drizzle the canola oil over the top. Sprinkle with the bread crumb mixture and toss to coat.

3. Transfer the Brussels sprouts to the prepared basket.

4. Place the basket on the toast position.

5. Select Toast, set temperature to 400°F (205°C), and set time to 15 minutes. Stir the Brussels a few times during cooking.

6. When cooking is complete, the Brussels sprouts should be lightly browned and crisp. Transfer the Brussels sprouts to a plate and sprinkle the sage on top before serving.

Nutrition: Calories 206 Carbs 0.1g Fat 2.8g Protein 10.8g

40. Air fryer Minestrone Soup

Preparation Time: 10 minutes

Cooking Time: 35 minutes

Servings: 6

Ingredients:

- 2 tablespoons olive oil
- 3 cloves garlic, minced
- 1 onion, diced
- 2 carrots, peeled and diced
- 2 celery stalks, diced
- 1 ½ teaspoons fresh basil
- 1 teaspoon dried oregano
- ½ teaspoon fennel seed
- 6 cups low-sodium chicken broth
- 28 ounce can tomatoes, diced
- 1 can kidney beans, drained and rinsed
- 1 zucchini, chopped
- 1 Parmesan rind
- 1 bay leaf
- 1 bunch kale, chopped and stems removed
- 2 teaspoons red wine vinegar
- kosher salt and freshly ground black pepper

- ⅓ cup Parmesan, grated

- 2 tablespoons fresh parsley leaves, chopped

Directions:

1. Set air fryer to saute, add olive oil, garlic, onion, carrots, and celery. Cook, occasionally stirring, until tender. Stir in basil, oregano, and fennel seeds, for a minute, until fragrant.

2. Pour in the chicken stock, tomatoes, kidney beans, zucchini, parmesan rind, and bay leaf. Select the manual high pressure setting and set for 5 minutes.

3. When completed, press quick release to remove all pressure.

4. Stir in the kale for about 2 minutes, then stir in red wine vinegar and season with salt and pepper to taste. Ready to serve.

Nutrition: Calories – 227 Protein – 14 g. Fat – 7 g. Carbs – 26 g.

41.   Air fryer Greek Beef Stew

Preparation Time: 15 minutes

Cooking Time: 40 minutes

Servings: 4

Ingredients:

- 1 ½ pounds stew beef cut into small cubes

- ¼ cup of butter

- 8 small onions

- 8 small potatoes

- 2-3 carrots, sliced

- ¾ cups tomato paste

- 1 teaspoon cinnamon

Directions:

1. Set air fryer to saute mode and cook beef in the butter until browned. This will take about 5 minutes. Then remove.

2. Put in the onions to the pot and saute about 5 minutes.

3. Stop saute mode. Add beef back to the pot and then add carrots, potatoes, tomato paste, and cinnamon. Add 2-3 cups of water.

4. Lock the lid and set pressure to high and cook for 35 minutes.

5. Allow steam to release naturally for 10 minutes and then quick release remaining pressure.

6. Ready to serve.

Nutrition: Calories – 479 Protein – 43 g. Fat – 20 g. Carbs – 31 g.

42. Air fryer Bean Soup

Preparation Time: 20 minutes

Cooking Time: 1 hour and 25 minutes

Servings: 6

Ingredients:

- 1 pound white beans
- 1 ¼ pound of beef shanks with bone
- 1 white onion, chopped
- 1 green bell pepper, chopped
- 2 carrots, chopped
- 4 tablespoons olive oil
- 2 tablespoons fresh parsley, chopped
- ½ teaspoon garlic, minced
- ½ tablespoon salt
- 1 can tomatoes, diced
- 1 liter water
- 3 bay leaves
- ½ teaspoon paprika

Directions:

1. Immerse beans in a bowl of cold water overnight.
2. Place the beef shanks and olive oil in air fryer and turn on saute setting. Brown on both sides

3. Remove the beans from water, and rinse. Add beans, diced tomatoes, paprika, bay leaves, and garlic.

4. Add water, close the lid, and cook on the manual high setting for 1 hour. Make sure the beans are soft, and if not, cook for another 30 minutes. Serve.

Nutrition: Calories – 86 Protein – 2.8 g. Fat – 5 g. Carbs – 9.7 g.

Snack & Dessert

43. Cheesy Garlic Sweet Potatoes

Preparation Time: 10 minutes

Cooking Time: 25 minutes

Servings: 4

Ingredients:

- Sea salt

- ¼ cup garlic butter melts

- ¾ cup shredded mozzarella cheese

- ½ cup of parmesan cheese freshly grated

- 4 medium sized sweet potatoes

- 2 tsp freshly chopped parsley

Directions:

1. Heat the oven to 400 degrees Fahrenheit and brush the potatoes with garlic butter and season each with pepper and salt. Arrange the cut side down on a greased baking sheet until the flesh is tender or they turn golden brown.

2. Remove them from the oven, flip the cut side up and top up with parsley and parmesan cheese.

3. Change the settings of your fryer oven to broil and on medium heat add the cheese and melt it. Sprinkle salt and pepper to taste. Serve them warm

Nutrition: Calories 321 Fat 9g, Carbs 13g Proteins 5g,

44. Crispy Garlic Baked Potato Wedges

Preparation Time: 5 minutes

Cooking Time: 10 minutes

Servings: 3

Ingredients:

- 3 tsp salt

- 1 tsp minced garlic

- 6 large russets

- ¼ cup olive oil

- 1 tsp paprika

- 2/3 finely grated parmesan cheese

- 2 tsp freshly chopped parsley

Directions:

1. Preheat the oven into 350 degrees Fahrenheit and line the baking sheet with a parchment pepper.

2. Cut the potatoes into halfway length and cut each half in half lengthways again. Make 8 wedges.

3. In small jug combine garlic, oil, paprika and salt and place your wedges in the baking sheets. Pour the oil mixture over the potatoes and toss them to ensure that they are evenly coated.

4. Arrange the potato wedges in a single layer on the baking tray and sprinkle salt and parmesan cheese if needed. Bake it for 35 minutes turning the wedges once half side is cooked. Flip the other side until they are both golden brown. Sprinkle parsley and the remaining parmesan before serving.

Nutrition: Calories, 289 Fat 6g Carbs 8g Proteins 2g

45.   Sticky Chicken Thai Wings

Preparation Time: 10 minutes

Cooking Time:30 minutes

Servings: 6

Ingredients:

- 3 pounds chicken wings removed

- 1 tsp sea salt to taste

For the glaze:

- ¾ cup Thai sweet chili sauce

- ¼ cup soy sauce

- 4 tsp brown sugar

- 4 tsp rice wine vinegar

- 3 tsp fish sauce

- 2 tsp lime juice

- 1 tsp lemon grass minced

- 2 tsp sesame oil

- 1 tsp garlic minced

Directions:

1. Preheat the oven to 350 degrees Fahrenheit. Lightly spray your baking tray with cooking tray and set it aside. To prepare the glaze combine the ingredients in a small bowl and whisk them until they are well combined. Pour half of the mixture into a pan and reserve the rest.

2. Trim any excess skin off the wing edges and season it with pepper and salt. Add the wings to a baking tray and pour the sauce over the wings tossing them for the sauce to evenly coat. Arrange them in a single layer and bake them for 15 minutes

3. While the wings are in the oven, bring your glaze to simmer in medium heat until there are visible bubbles.

4. Once the wings are cooled on one side rotate each piece and Bake it for an extra 10 minutes baste them and return them into the oven to allow for more cooking until they are golden brown. Garnish with onion slices, cilantro, chili flakes. Sprinkle the remaining salt. Serve it with glaze of your choice.

Nutrition: Calories 246 Fat 16g Carbs 19g Proteins: 20g

46.   Coconut Shrimp

Preparation Time: 15 minutes

Cooking Time: 15 minutes

Servings: 6

Ingredients:

- Salt and pepper

- 1-pound jumbo shrimp peeled and deveined

- ½ cup all-purpose flour

- For batter:

- ½ cup beer

- 1 tsp baking powder

- ½ cup all-purpose flour

- 1 egg

- For coating:

- 1 cup panko bread crumbs

- 1 cup shredded coconut

Directions:

1. Line the baking tray with parchment paper. In a shallow bowl add ½ cup flour for dredging and in another bowl whisk the batter ingredients. The batter should resemble a pancake consistency. If it is too thick add a little mineral or beer whisking in between. In another bowl mix together the shredded coconut and bread crumbs.

2. Dredge the shrimp in flour shaking off any excess before dipping in the batter and coat it with bread crumb mixture. Lightly press the coconut into the shrimp. Place them into the baking sheet and repeat the process until you have several.

3. In a Dutch oven skillet heat vegetable oil until it is nice and hot fry the frozen shrimp batches for 3 minutes per side. Dry out them on a paper towel lined plate. Serve immediately with sweet chili sauce.

Nutrition: Calories 287 Fat 11g Carbs 46g Proteins 30g

47. Spicy Korean Cauliflower Bites

Preparation Time: 15 minutes

Cooking Time:30 minutes

Servings: 4

Ingredients:

- 2 eggs

- 1 lb. cauliflower

- 2/3 cups of corn starch

- 2 tsp smoked paprika

- 1 tsp garlic grated

- 1 tsp ginger grated

- 1 lb. panko

- 1 tsp sea salt

For the Korean barbecue sauce

- 1 cup ketchup

- ½ cup Korea chili flakes

- ½ cup minced garlic

- ½ cup red pepper

Directions:

1. Cut the cauliflower into small sizes based on your taste and preference.

2. In a small bowl add cornstarch and eggs and mix them until they are smooth.

3. Add onions, garlic, ginger, smoked paprika and coat them with panko.

4. Apply some pressure so that the panko can stick and repeat this with all the cauliflower.

5. Set your Air Fryer Oven to 400 degrees Fahrenheit for a half an hour. Line your tray with aluminum foil or parchment paper and use nonstick spray to cover it.

6. When the air fryer BEEPS 'add food' put your food and set the timer to 30 minutes or choose a program that will automatically choose the duration the food will take to cook. In the middle of the cooking the appliance will beep again to indicate turn food. You will take it out and flip it for the other side to cook well.

7. While it is cooking for the second part you can begin preparing your spicy Korean barbecue sauce.

8. Sauté the ingredients and Drizzle with the oil at the bottom. Fry the garlic for a minute before adding all the remaining ingredients and simmering it for 15 minutes

9. Keep it warm and serve with your cauliflower bites.

Nutrition: Calories 118 Fat 2g Carbs 21g Proteins 4g

48.   Mini Popovers

Preparation Time: 10 minutes

Cooking Time: 15 minutes

Servings: 4

Ingredients:

- 1 tsp butter melted

- 2 eggs at room temperature

- 1 cup of milk at room temperature

- 1 cup all-purpose flour

- Salt and pepper to taste

Directions:

1. Generously coat a mini popover with nonstick spray.

2. Add all the ingredients to a blender and process it at medium speed.

3. Fill each mold with 2 tsp batter. Place a drip pan at the bottom of the cooking chamber.

4. Using the display panel selects AIRFRY and adjusts it to 400 degrees Fahrenheit and a time of 20 minutes then touch START.

5. When the display panel indicates 'add food' place the egg bite mold on the lower side of the cooking tray. When the display indicates "TURNFOOD" do not touch anything. When the popovers are brown open the cooking chamber and pierce them to release steam and cook for a minute or so.

6. Serve immediately.

Nutrition: Calories53 Fat 1g Carbs 9g Proteins 2g

49.   Lemon Pear Compote

Preparation Time: 10 minutes

Cooking Time: 15 minutes

Servings: 6

Ingredients:

- 3 cups pears, cored and cut into chunks

- 1 tsp vanilla

- 1 tsp liquid stevia

- 1 tbsp. lemon zest, grated

- 2 tbsp. lemon juice

Directions:

1. Put all of the ingredients in the inner pot of air fryer and stir well.

2. Seal pot and cook on high for 15 minutes.

3. As soon as the cooking is done, let it release pressure naturally for 10 minutes then release remaining using quick release. Remove lid.

4. Stir and serve.

Nutrition: Calories – 50 Protein – 0.4 g. Fat – 0.2 g. Carbs – 12.7 g.

50.   Strawberry Stew

Preparation Time: 10 minutes

Cooking Time: 15 minutes

Servings: 4

Ingredients:

- 12 oz fresh strawberries, sliced

- 1 tsp vanilla

- 1 1/2 cups water

- 1 tsp liquid stevia

- 2 tbsp. lime juice

Directions:

1. Put all of the ingredients in the inner pot of air fryer and stir well.

2. Seal pot and cook on high for 15 minutes.

3. As soon as the cooking is done, let it release pressure naturally for 10 minutes then release remaining using quick release. Remove lid.

4. Stir and serve.

Nutrition: Calories – 36 Protein – 0.7 g. Fat – 0.3 g. Carbs – 8.5 g.

Measurement Conversion Chart

CONVERSION CHART

Liquid Measure		**Dry Measure**		**Linear Measure**	
8 ounces =	1 cup	2 pints =	1 quart	12 inches =	1 foot
2 cups =	1 pint	4 quarts =	1 gallon	3 feet =	1 yard
16 ounces =	1 pint	8 quarts =	2 gallons or 1 peck	5.5 yards =	1 rod
4 cups =	1 quart			40 rods =	1 furlong
1 gill =	1/2 cup or 1/4 pint	4 pecks =	8 gallons or 1 bushel	8 furlongs (5280 feet) =	1 mile
2 pints =	1 quart	16 ounces =	1 pound	6080 feet =	1 nautical mile
4 quarts =	1 gallon	2000 lbs. =	1 ton		
31.5 gal. =	1 barrel				

		Conversion of US Weight and Mass Measure to Metric System		*Conversion of US Linear Measure to Metric System*	
3 tsp =	1 tbsp			1 inch =	2.54 centimeters
2 tbsp =	1/8 cup or 1 fluid ounce	.0353 ounces =	1 gram		
4 tbsp =	1/4 cup	1/4 ounce =	7 grams	1 foot =	.3048 meters
8 tbsp =	1/2 cup	1 ounce =	28.35 grams	1 yard =	.9144 meters
1 pinch =	1/8 tsp or less	4 ounces =	113.4 grams	1 mile =	1609.3 meters or 1.6093 kilometers
1 tsp =	60 drops	8 ounces =	226.8 grams		
		1 pound =	454 grams		
Conversion of US Liquid Measure to Metric System		2.2046 pounds =	1 kilogram	.03937 in. =	1 millimeter
		.98421 long ton or 1.1023 short tons =	1 metric ton	.3937 in.=	1 centimeter
1 fluid oz. =	29.573 milliliters			3.937 in.=	1 decimeter
1 cup =	230 milliliters			39.37 in.=	1 meter
1 quart =	.94635 liters			3280.8 ft. or .62137 miles =	1 kilometer
1 gallon =	3.7854 liters				
.033814 fluid ounce =	1 milliliter				
3.3814 fluid ounces =	1 deciliter				
33.814 fluid oz. or 1.0567 qt. =	1 liter				

To convert a Fahrenheit temperature to Centigrade, do the following:
a. Subtract 32   b. Multiply by 5   c. Divide by 9

To convert Centigrade to Fahrenheit, do the following:
a. Multiply by 9   b. Divide by 5   c. Add 32

AIR FRYER COOKING TIMES

	Temperature (°F)	Time (min)		Temperature (°F)	Time (min)
Vegetables					
Asparagus (sliced 1-inch)	400°F	5	Onions (pearl)	400°F	10
Beets (whole)	400°F	40	Parsnips (½-inch chunks)	380°F	15
Broccoli (florets)	400°F	6	Peppers (1-inch chunks)	400°F	15
Brussels Sprouts (halved)	380°F	15	Potatoes (small baby, 1.5 lbs)	400°F	15
Carrots (sliced ½-inch)	380°F	15	Potatoes (1-inch chunks)	400°F	12
Cauliflower (florets)	400°F	12	Potatoes (baked whole)	400°F	40
Corn on the cob	390°F	6	Squash (½-inch chunks)	400°F	12
Eggplant (1½-inch cubes)	400°F	15	Sweet Potato (baked)	380°F	30 to 35
Fennel (quartered)	370°F	15	Tomatoes (cherry)	400°F	4
Green Beans	400°F	5	Tomatoes (halves)	350°F	10
Kale leaves	250°F	12	Zucchini (½-inch sticks)	400°F	12
Mushrooms (sliced ¼-inch)	400°F	5			
Chicken					
Breasts, bone in (1.25 lbs.)	370°F	25	Legs, bone in (1.75 lbs.)	380°F	30
Breasts, boneless (4 oz.)	380°F	12	Wings (2 lbs.)	400°F	12
Drumsticks (2.5 lbs.)	370°F	20	Game Hen (halved - 2 lbs.)	390°F	20
Thighs, bone in (2 lbs.)	380°F	22	Whole Chicken (6.5 lbs.)	360°F	75
Thighs, boneless (1.5 lbs.)	380°F	18 to 20	Tenders	360°F	8 to 10
Beef					
Burger (4 oz.)	370°F	16 to 20	Meatballs (3-inch)	380°F	10
Filet Mignon (8 oz.)	400°F	18	Ribeye, bone in (1-inch, 8 oz.)	400°F	10 to 15
Flank Steak (1.5 lbs.)	400°F	12	Sirloin steaks (1-inch, 12 oz.)	400°F	9 to 14
London Broil (2 lbs.)	400°F	20 to 28	Beef Eye Round Roast (4 lbs.)	390°F	45 to 55
Meatballs (1-inch)	380°F	7			
Pork and Lamb					
Loin (2 lbs.)	360°F	55	Bacon (thick cut)	400°F	6 to 10
Pork Chops, bone in (1-inch, 6.5 oz.)	400°F	12	Sausages	380°F	15
Tenderloin (1 lb.)	370°F	15	Lamb Loin Chops (1-inch thick)	400°F	8 to 12
Bacon (regular)	400°F	5 to 7	Rack of lamb (1.5 - 2 lbs.)	380°F	22
Fish and Seafood					
Calamari (8 oz.)	400°F	4	Tuna steak	400°F	7 to 10
Fish Fillet (1-inch, 8 oz.)	400°F	10	Scallops	400°F	5 to 7
Salmon, fillet (6 oz.)	380°F	12	Shrimp	400°F	5
Swordfish steak	400°F	10			

Lightning Source UK Ltd.
Milton Keynes UK
UKHW020634280521
384530UK00001B/82

9 781802 937930